A GUIDE
TO THE THEMES
FROM *PREPARE*

A GUIDE
TO THE THEMES
FROM *PREPARE*

J. Paul Nyquist

MOODY PUBLISHERS

CHICAGO

Developed by James Vincent
Interior design: Ragont Design
Cover design: Erik M. Peterson

ISBN: 978-0-8024-1458-8

We hope you enjoy this book from Moody Publishers. Our goal is to provide high-quality, thought-provoking books and products that connect truth to your real needs and challenges. For more information on other books and products written and produced from a biblical perspective, go to www.moodypublishers.com or write to:

Moody Publishers
820 N. LaSalle Boulevard
Chicago, IL 60610

1 3 5 7 9 10 8 6 4 2

Printed in the United States of America

CONTENTS

ABOUT THIS GUIDE

This guide to the book *Prepare,* by J. Paul Nyquist, is published in response to many readers of the book who have wanted to discuss its ideas and apply its themes to their lives. The topics of *Prepare* continue to remain timely to Christians in America and abroad, where opposition to the Christian faith and lifestyle has become increasingly apparent. Both Dr. Nyquist and the publisher of *Prepare* (Moody Publishers, 2015) desire that this study guide will help you grow strong in your faith as well as confident in God the Father and Jesus the Son and Savior in trying times. Let's remember such times offer great opportunity to honor Christ as we declare the good news of salvation and demonstrate His compassion to those who oppose us.

This Guide is equally useful for small-group discussion and private study of *Prepare.* The first section of each chapter, titled "The Issues," will help readers consider key themes associated with living their faith in a hostile culture. "The Issues" includes brief summaries of key ideas, each followed by one or two questions that help you explore truths in the book and better understand and apply them to your life. Some of the questions enable you to look at key Bible verses from the chapter in more detail, again to understand them better and apply them to your life.

The second section, "Ponder and Discuss," highlights (in italics) key statements in the chapter worthy of further reflection and application. The questions are intended to spark discussion. If you are using this guide for private study, the questions should enable you to see action steps to take personally and should enliven your prayer times and personal study of the Scriptures.

The goal of this guide is to give each reader of *Prepare* a deeper understanding of the resources at our disposal as opposition and even persecution are encountered in this hostile world. There is confidence, peace, and even joy as we serve our God steadfastly. And as noted in several chapters, when we are prepared to love and serve in a hostile world, our godly responses to persecution will both surprise those who oppose us and offer us opportunities to present our Christian faith. May all of this bring honor to Christ, our Savior.

INTRODUCTION

———

THE ISSUES

Houston city officials in 2014 ordered five area pastors to surrender all sermons, emails, and text messages that mentioned homosexuality, gender issues, or Mayor Annise Parker. The springboard for their subpoena of these documents was a successful petition drive, signed by church members and others, to create a public referendum on a new city law called the Houston Equal Rights Ordinance.

1. What issues are involved when church members sign petitions and file a lawsuit when the necessary petitions are rejected? Do you believe Christians have a right to be involved this way in politics?

2. If you were a member of the church and learned your pastor's messages were being examined by the city, how would you react? If you were a ministry leader at one of those five Houston churches, how would you feel?

John S. Dickerson predicts the rate of cultural change in America will accelerate "as the oldest two generations die, taking their traditional values and votes with them." Another respected pastor, Erwin Lutzer, declares much of our Judeo-Christian heritage is already gone, replaced by "an intolerant form of humanism." He concludes, "The cultural war we used to speak about appears to be over, and we have lost."

3. If these two pastors are correct, these are dire warnings for followers of Jesus. To what extent do you think they are right —is this overstating the situation? Give reasons for your conclusion.

Christianity Today reported that although martyrdoms doubled in 2013, "most persecution is not violence. It's a 'squeeze' [or pressuring] of Christians in one of five spheres of life: private, family, community, national, and church."

4. Although death is typically painful and certainly final, there is much suffering in threats, personal estrangement, and isolation from one's family, community, and church. Which would be most difficult for you to accept, and why?

PONDER AND DISCUSS

For nearly 250 years, Christians in America were able to live in relative freedom from persecution. . . .
But we're witnessing an epic change in our culture—a spiritual climate shift threatening to reshape life as we know it. Hostility and intolerance are replacing toleration. Rejection and even hatred are pushing aside acceptance.

1. What examples of rejection, hostility, intolerance or even hatred have you or some Christian you know experienced in the past that would support this claim?

Despite more frequent episodes of persecution many American citizens have not personally experienced suffering for standing for their faith and Christian values. Dr. Nyquist compares our situation with that of the disciples prior to Christ's march to the cross:

Christ predicted persecution as His disciples struggled with the requirements of following Him. . . . He reminded them the world would "hate them just as it has hated Me." I suspect until the Passion Week the disciples were much like us—they heard Jesus' words and sought to understand them. But until they were actually experiencing these truths, the disciples—like us—couldn't quite connect with what their Teacher was saying. Events in the book of Acts quickly remedied that.

2. After reading the introduction to *Prepare*, do you think that Jesus' warnings are relevant and applicable to the time we are currently living in? Explain why or why not.

PART ONE

The New Reality

1

AWAKENING TO A DIFFERENT WORLD

THE ISSUES

The Definition of Marriage

Dr. Nyquist explores "four game-changing developments" that demonstrate that Christian tenets have been challenged and dismissed by American society. The first is the abandonment of biblical marriage through three key decisions of the U.S. Supreme Court: (1) dismissing in 2013 the Defense of Marriage Act (DOMA) that defined marriage as one man and one woman; (2) refusing in 2014 to hear appeals of five states, reinforcing the national scope of the decision; and more recently (3) the 2015 decision declaring the right of same-sex couples to marry "is part of the liberty promised by the Fourteenth Amendment."

1. Consider the definition of marriage offered by DOMA and originating in the Bible (Gen. 2:23)—a union between one man and one woman—and that of the Supreme Court—two persons. What are two or three reasons the first definition is more accurate? What could you say to someone who prefers the definition given by the court?

Same-Sex Marriage and Religious Liberty

The second development is the government's erosion of Christian freedom. Three classic examples involve a baker, a florist, and a photographer (from three different states) who refused to provide wedding services to a same-sex couple because of the vendors' religious belief that marriage is between a man and a woman. They faced ridicule, boycotts, and state sanctions because of their opposition. One closed her shop. The Religious Freedom Restoration Act did not protect them as individuals.

2. Should we expect the government to protect individual merchants and businesspeople who refuse to provide their services for activities they do not believe in? Why or why not?

3. If you were (or are) a baker, florist, or photographer, would you refuse to cater or provide services for a same-sex wedding? What if you were faced with government fines or penalties as a result of your refusal?

The third development is special considerations given to special interest groups, including those in the LGBT community. Laws could require religious nonprofit organizations and Christian colleges and universities to hire gay and transgender individuals as part of "nondiscriminatory" hiring.

4. The community standards of a Christian college, typically guided by biblical principles, often lead to a code of conduct. In the case of Gordon College, what is the most compelling argument its leaders can offer for not adding to its staff members of the LGBT community? What can they do to respond with love and grace and still honor the Scriptures?

Anti-Christian Hostility

The fourth development is outright hostility toward Christianity.

5. Mike Adams was a tenured professor and received two faculty awards and strong reviews. Yet he was denied promotion to full professor when he spoke about his faith. He won his day in court, being awarded his professorship with back pay. That was justice, but often justice does not take place. If you were in a situation at work where you were told not to read your Bible or pray alone during breaks or else risk demotion, what would you do? Why?

6. Five incidents of antagonistic actions against individuals and groups are listed on the final page of the chapter. Which one of these is most disturbing to you and why?

PONDER AND DISCUSS

But despite efforts to equate the discrimination against the LGBT community with the enslavement of African Americans, the issues are fundamentally different. While there's nothing sinful about having black or white skin, the Bible says homosexual behavior and changing one's gender is wrong—an affront to the Creator (Lev. 18:22; 20:13; Rom. 1:26–27).

1. Do you agree with this argument? Why or why not?

2. What is the challenge of presenting this argument to someone who says that truth is relative—"It's your truth, not mine"? How could you present this reality to someone who questions that sin exists, or that God exists?

2

CROSSING THE RUBICON

THE ISSUES

Cultural Decay

Dr. Nyquist describes this chapter as "a cultural postmortem" on how America became a "highly individualized, relativistic, anti-Christian culture." A literal postmortem is an examination of the deceased to determine the cause or causes of death. A figurative postmortem examines causes that contributed to the demise or failure of a project or institution.

1. Do you consider all Christian values to be wholly rejected by American society at large? Or to put it another way, is "Christian America" dead, a relic of the past? Explain why or why not.

Change in a culture takes place over time and follows a five-step process: (1) A contact happens, (2) a champion emerges, (3) a coalition builds, (4) a law is passed, and (5) integration occurs. Each cultural change follows this cyclical movement that influences key issues and how and why people do things. The cycle is reproduced below:

CULTURAL CHANGE CYCLE

2. A coalition must be gained (step 3) to reach "a tipping point" where a law is advocated or challenged that leads to cultural change. This is when debate between the coalition for change and its opponents takes place. In what ways can Christian citizens influence the argument before and during the coalition's growth? Discuss how this can be done publicly and privately.

3. Why do you think many Christians have declined to be involved in these approaches—both by outward actions and private prayers?

Nyquist traces the five-step process of cultural change that has occurred regarding the nature of religious freedom through legal interpretations of the "establishment of religion" clause in the Constitution's First Amendment. Under step four, he summarizes seven laws spanning fifty-one years (1962–2013). He begins with the case *Engel v. Vitale*, in which the Supreme Court ruled that prayer and Bible reading in public schools violate the establishment of religion clause. He ends with *United States v. Windsor*, which ruled the Defense of Marriage Act (marriage is only between one man and one woman) as unconstitutional.

4. Nyquist argues that the Supreme Court's removal of religious influence in the making of laws has led to a slippery slope of laws redefined that allow abortions to minors and marriage to any two adult persons. How important are religious principles to establishing and maintaining laws? To what extent should high-court judges weigh religious commands, which English legal scholar William Blackstone regarded as "binding over all the globe, in all countries, and at all times" (p. 43)?

Liberty and Worldview

In the case of *Planned Parenthood v. Casey*, the Supreme Court extended the constitutional right to liberty to a personal understanding, writing "At the heart of liberty is the right to define one's own concept of existence, of meaning, of the universe, and of the mystery of human life."

5. What are the dangers of making liberty subject to one's personal concept of existence and meaning?

PONDER AND DISCUSS

Is gay marriage the logical end to our cultural change? With privacy and individualism reigning supreme in our courts, and with a relativistic philosophy devoid of absolutes dominating individuals around the country, what else could we see in this country in the name of marriage? Is polygamy wrong? Is incest out of the question?

1. The final two questions above are rhetorical in nature, assuming the answers are both no, or at least not necessarily. Do you think Dr. Nyquist is being alarmist, or is that a possibility? Defend your answer and discuss it with others.

2. What response could you give to those who would say, "In the privacy of your home it is okay" (which is the argument that overturned sodomy laws in America [*Lawrence v. Texas*])?

PART TWO

Understanding Persecution— Five Counterintuitive Principles

3

NORMAL NOT
STRANGE

THE ISSUES

Christ's Suffering

The two disciples who did not recognize Jesus as He walked with them toward the village of Emmaus also did not recognize that Jesus had to suffer great pain and death, both to fulfill prophecy and to accomplish spiritual redemption.

1. Most Christians think of Christ's severe yet essential suffering only when they participate in a Communion service at church. What other times, if any, do you think about the suffering and death of Jesus?

2. Most believers in Jesus as the Savior sent to deliver the human race prefer to think of Him as the reigning King rather than the suffering Messiah. Is that the right emphasis (cf. Luke 24:26)? What are the benefits of remembering Jesus' suffering on the cross?

Christians and the World

Jesus warned His followers of the world—not planet earth, but the personal world we encounter, that is, the beliefs and values of prevailing society. That world is antagonistic to God and His Word, and its citizens hate Christians because they (1) are different, (2) bear Christ's name, and (3) expose sin.

3. Dr. Nyquist notes that the world loves "those who identify with, conform to, and embrace its values. . . . But if we don't conform to the world . . . the world has zero tolerance for us." Can Christians still conform to this world and thus be no different than people of the world? (Consider Romans 8:2 as you answer this question.)

4. How would our conformity with the world's system influence the degree we would experience rejection and persecution?

5. Those who renounce the world's system, refusing to conform to its expectations and values, become disciples. Discipleship, writes, Dr. Nyquist, requires that a person (1) renounces self, (2) sacrifices self, and (3) keeps following Jesus. Which of these three elements of a disciple is the most difficult for you to embrace? Why?

PONDER AND DISCUSS

One of the most difficult truths for us to grasp is that the world hates us. The world doesn't tolerate us—even though toleration is a supposed value of our society. It doesn't like us. No, it hates us.

1. That is a hard truth to hear and to accept. No one likes to be despised or subjected to rejection. Yet three times in two verses (John 15:18–19) Jesus declares the world hates His followers. What is your reaction to being told you can expect hatred for your faith? Be honest about your feelings, which could be shock, surprise, fear, or hesitancy ("What did I get myself into by following Jesus?"), or all of these.

2. Jesus says we should not be surprised by such animosity, because "if they persecuted me, they will also persecute you" (v. 20). What is your reaction to being told that hatred may be expressed in the form of *persecution*?

3. What steps can you take to prepare for the rejection and persecution that may come your way?

Beloved, do not be surprised at the fiery trial when it comes upon you to test you, as though something strange were happening to you (1 Peter 4:12). *As American Christians, we . . . don't expect suffering and persecution. . . . Living in a culture with Judeo-Christian roots, we expect our lives to be marked by general prosperity and societal acceptance. Persecution is strange.*

4. Part 2 of *Prepare* includes five seemingly paradoxical statements. Nyquist calls these "five counterintuitive biblical principles" for understanding persecution. Because they seem to contradict expectations and perhaps logic as well, they are hard to accept as reality. Consider the first one: "Persecution is normal, not strange." Why is it hard to accept that persecution is a normal prospect for a Christian? Consider where you live, personal experiences, things you were taught growing up, and any other factors that may influence your questioning that persecution is normal.

4

BLESSED NOT CURSED

THE ISSUES

The Blessing of Persecution

Nyquist offers the testimonies of three men who would suffer greatly that persecution means you're blessed not cursed: the apostles Peter (1 Peter 3:14) and James (James 1:12) and the Master Himself, Jesus (Matt. 5:10).

1. Consider both the verb *blessed* and the noun *blessing*. Most uses of the word in either form are associated with opportunities, good outcomes, receiving something unexpected or in abundance, even deliverance from a threat or trouble. Can you think of a blessing, i.e., positive outcome, that you, a friend, or a family member received that at first was perceived to be a huge negative or devastating loss? Share it with your group. If you are doing a personal study, thank God in prayer for His wisdom in blessing you with a situation He used for your good. Either way, write down this example(s) so you can recall it the next time His blessing is not what you expected but is for your good.

Even when we come up with examples of blessings of ultimately good outcomes from seemingly bad situations, it is hard to see that eventual outcome during the initial pain or loss. In fact, that pain and/or loss may send your mind and emotions reeling.

2. In what ways can you look beyond your initial thoughts and feelings to recall and abide in the truth that persecution means you're blessed, not cursed? Consider the first paragraph under "The Issues" above for a couple of clues.

Persecution brings blessing in our lives in two key ways. First, it allows us to know Christ better, more intimately. The litany of troubles the apostle Paul experienced (2 Cor. 11:24–27) proved he suffered persecution as much as anyone in the early church. He looked at those trials and later contrasted them with his earthly accomplishments and titles (Phil. 3:5–7) and concluded his personal achievements were like rubbish. His goal was to intimately know Christ "and . . . share his sufferings, becoming like him in his death" (v. 10).

3. Dr. Nyquist writes that Paul acknowledged all things have value, but knowing Jesus as Lord of his life has greater value than his position and accomplishments. Why is that perspective so difficult for most Christians to accept? Why is this perspective so hard for *you* to accept?

4. Nyquist quotes Paul saying "Indeed, I count everything as loss because of the surpassing worth of knowing Christ Jesus my Lord" (Phil. 3:8), except Nyquist uses italics to emphasize "*my* Lord." What is the difference between calling Christ Jesus "the Lord" and calling Him "my Lord"? How does personal knowledge of a person differ from intellectual knowledge?

The second way persecution brings blessing in our lives is it allows us to become more like Christ. Read again James 1:2–4, where the apostle James tells members of the early church to regard their persecution with joy because "testing of your faith produces steadfastness . . . that you may be perfect and complete."

5. How can the discomfort and downright pain of persecution and suffering make us like Jesus in terms of character qualities? Since we cannot be perfect in terms of our sinful nature (1 John 1:8), in what way(s) can we become more like Jesus as we experience suffering?

PONDER AND DISCUSS

Clearly, American Christians have had it easy. We've not faced persecution on a regular basis like our brothers and sisters around the world. But that's about to change. A hostile culture is bringing persecution our way.

1. Do you agree that many people in America are hostile to Christianity and Christians? Why or why not?

2. Assume Nyquist's conclusion is correct: "A hostile culture is bringing persecution our way." In this chapter Dr. Nyquist gives two major reasons we should welcome persecution as a blessing: (1) Persecution allows us to know Christ better. (2) Persecution allows us to become more like Christ. Do these truths free you to welcome persecution? Discuss and defend your answer.

5

EXPOSED NOT PROTECTED

THE ISSUES

God and the Government

God appoints governmental rulers, who are to be servants of God and expected to punish evildoers and reward those who do good (1 Peter 2:14; Rom. 13:1–3). But in our fallen world, not all leaders regard themselves as servants nor punish evil as God declares it. Dr. Nyquist gives two examples of men threatened with death for doing good. The prophet Daniel was thrown to the lions when he refused to stop praying to God (Dan. 6:1–17), and Shadrach, Meshach, and Abednego were thrown into a blazing furnace when they refused to bow down to a tall golden image in worship of King Nebuchadnezzar (Dan. 3:1–23).

1. Read the Daniel 6 passage. Daniel knew about the law yet disobeyed it by praying to God three times each day (v. 10). Why did he disobey the law and the king if he was a loyal subject? What was the final outcome for Daniel and King Darius the morning after he entered the den of lions?

2. Read the Daniel 3 passage, especially the three men's response when threatened with death. Did they believe God would deliver them from the fire (compare vv. 17 and 18)?

The warning of this chapter is that followers of Christ often will be "exposed and not protected" from persecution. This exposure may even be at the hands of family members, as Jesus warned (Matt. 10:21). The closest example of that in America is the Civil War, when brothers and family members, divided in loyalties, abandoned and even fought each other.

3. Jesus said our beliefs will strain family relations—to the point that family members can become enemies (vv. 35–36). How difficult would that be for you? Why does Jesus say we must stand with Him, according to v. 37?

This chapter may be realistic, but it may not seem encouraging. In the final three sections—the first two on family and friends leaving us and the third on being exposed and vulnerable—the following words describe our situation: *hostility, betrayal, isolation, lonely, hopeless, abandoned, alone, unjust persecution*, and *unfair punishment*. But as a realistic warning, it is important medicine administered by Jesus Himself (in Matt. 10:22, 35–37).

4. How do the words of Jesus—about His compassion, love, and commitment to you—and the example of His life give you hope to be steadfast, to remain in Him rather than abandon Him?

PONDER AND DISCUSS

*Even though [Paul] remained in subjection to the governmental author-
ities his entire life as a faithful Roman citizen, he still was executed. And
he wasn't alone. . . . Believers were rounded up, tortured and fed to wild
beasts in the Coliseum or covered with pitch and lit as torches for parties.
. . . A march through church history reveals a long and sordid array of
government-sponsored persecutions.*

1. The attacks on Christians in the first centuries after Jesus'
   ascension were grisly and barbaric, but suffering short of
   death can be just as intimidating. What kinds of social,
   economic, or emotional suffering have Christians faced
   recently or could they face in the coming years if accused—
   or even convicted—of bigotry or hatred for opposing
   governmental laws they believe violate God's prevailing laws?

2. What if you, like these believers in the past and believers in
   some Middle Eastern countries today, were faced with the
   threat of a violent death as punishment for your faith unless
   you renounced Christ? How do you think you would react
   and respond in that situation—with confidence or hesitation,
   peace or panic, forbearance or retaliation, conviction or
   capitulation? Why do you think you would react like this
   if faced with this ultimatum? Is how you think you *would*
   respond different from how you think you *should* respond? If
   so, what can you do to prepare your heart now in case we are
   faced with a death-defying situation in the future?

Reread the testimony of one angel and the words of two dedicated servants of God:

The Most High rules the kingdom of men and gives it to whom he will and sets over it the lowliest of men. . . . For there is no authority except from God, and those that exist have been instituted by God. . . . You would have no authority over me at all unless it had been given you from above. (Dan. 4:17; Rom. 13:1; John 19:11)

3. The Scriptures clearly reveal that rulers are given authority by God and are subject to God's authority. What should be our attitude toward those rulers and governmental leaders, knowing God has ultimately placed them in their positions and they will be accountable to God for their decisions? How can this give you both hope and courage for future laws that may result in persecution?

4. What is your current attitude toward leaders with whom you disagree? If it does not coincide with the truth that a sovereign God has placed these leaders in their position of authority, confess that to God. Seek to respect them as leaders even if you must oppose their policies by words and actions.

6

COMPASSION NOT ANGER

THE ISSUES

Loving Our Enemies

One definition of an enemy is "one not loved." Yet Jesus says to His followers, "Love your enemies and pray for those who persecute you" (Matt. 5:44). This seems a great paradox: How can you love someone who is not loved and who is hostile to you?

1. Try to answer the above question. How can you and I love someone who is hostile? Our answer should be based on biblical principles of who Jesus is, what He has done, and the resources we have in God the Father, God the Son, and God the Holy Spirit.

Christians are not only to love and pray for their enemies but to "bless those who persecute" them. We are to "bless and . . . not curse them" (Rom. 12:14).

2. What does it mean to bless someone, according to Nyquist? What does it mean to curse someone?

As Christians, our blessing of an enemy should extend beyond prayers on their behalf to actions, including hospitality and help in needs they have (see Rom. 12:20). Such actions come from a heart of compassion.

3. Authentic love will result in compassionate action. Besides showing hospitality, from bringing your enemy something he or she can use to inviting the person over for a dessert, what other actions can you take?

The key reason we honor our enemies is to speak on behalf of our Savior, while "being prepared to make a defense to anyone who asks you for a reason for the hope that is in you" (1 Peter 3:15). When we "bless our enemies instead of cursing them . . . they will ask us about it," Dr. Nyquist writes. "They will bring it up because they are curious or furious."

4. If you spend enough time displaying compassion to an enemy, he or she will notice and wonder why, responding either with curiosity or fury. We probably welcome their curious questions but fear their potential anger. What can you do ahead of time to prepare for those who attack you as insincere or trying to make them look bad? (One way, of course, is to keep in mind "the hope that is in you.")

PONDER AND DISCUSS

The New Testament's teaching is clear, although it cuts against the grain of our emotions. Jesus, Paul, and Peter all echo the same command: Respond to your persecutors with compassion, not anger.

1. Do you think you are at the point where you believe you can pray for someone who is hostile to you? If the answer is no, what do you think you need to do to reach that point?

2. Are you at the point where you also can demonstrate compassion toward the person, to the point of doing good deeds on behalf of this individual? Be honest. If you are not able to show compassion, ask God to reveal why. If you do know why, ask God to change your attitude.
   If you are in a group, give your answer. If you are unable to show compassion, tell the group why you are struggling with this attitude of compassion. (Later, alone, admit this to God and ask for His strength to move toward compassion.)

7

REWARDED NOT FORGOTTEN

THE ISSUES

Rewards for Faithfulness

This chapter looks at the rewards we may receive in heaven for our faithfulness on earth. Some say rewards don't matter, as we will simply throw them at the feet of Jesus in gratitude or be happy just to be in heaven with God the Father and Jesus, the King of Kings.

1. Did the description of various rewards given in heaven strike you as a selfish motive for living for Jesus? Why or why not?

2. Does the prospect of rewards encourage you to keep on serving Jesus? Explain your answer.

A key passage declaring that Jesus will reward those who suffer persecution for His name is Matthew 5:11–12: "Blessed are you when others revile you and persecute you and utter all kinds of evil against you falsely on my account. Rejoice and be glad, for your reward is great in heaven, for so they persecuted the prophets who were before you."

3. Although this promise means God will set injustices right in heaven for those who suffered for doing good, it also means while on earth Christians will endure some or even much persecution for Jesus. Does that fact make you confused or perhaps upset that God now allows His people to suffer? Why or why not?

The writers of Hebrews and James both emphasize the need to persevere through persecution (Heb. 10:35–36; James 1:12). Nyquist adds, "It'll get hard, but we cannot and must not quit." The apostle James, who led the early church through much persecution, wrote "Blessed is the man who remains steadfast under trial, for when he has stood the test he will receive the crown of life, which God has promised to those who love him."

4. The "crown of life" is presented not to those who undergo persecution but those who remain steadfast in the trial. That means those who stand steady in their faith during persecution will be remembered and rewarded in heaven. What would you say to nonbelievers who might argue, "Justice delayed is not justice at all. Yours is not a fair God if He makes you suffer in this life only for a reward sometime in the distant future"?

PONDER AND DISCUSS

*James says a man is blessed if he "remains steadfast" in his trials.
... The brave steadfastness must continue until the ordeal ends. It doesn't
mean we'll never experience failure, but it requires us to right the ship,
confess the error, and refuse to surrender. Then we'll have stood the test.*

1. The fear of failing in one's faith is real. But God is not
   expecting us to be perfect, writes Nyquist, just to bring any
   failure to Him, confess it, and "refuse to surrender." Do you
   believe with God's help you can endure? If yes, how? If not,
   ask others to pray on your behalf, and ask God to give you a
   fuller vision of His compassion and ability through His Spirit
   to be faithful before Him.

*In a culture rapidly growing hostile to Christianity, we can predict how
Jesus' followers will be classified. We'll be the losers and outcasts perceived
useless to the greater culture—except as objects of hate deserving punishment and plundering. We'll feel forsaken because in an earthly, temporal
sense, we will be.*

2. Perhaps you have not experienced persecution, ridicule, or
   rejection that you can recall. But if you follow God's law and
   speak on His behalf, persecution will come. Being called a
   loser or being treated as an outcast by friends or family makes
   most people hesitate to defend what they believe. What

concepts in this chapter make it worth your while to be steadfast in your faith, not renouncing or ignoring your personal relationship with God through His Son, Jesus?

PART THREE

Reasons for Hope

8

GOD OUR HELP

THE ISSUES

Deliverance from Persecution

God can deliver His people, and often does—but not always. In the case of the three Hebrew men taken captive and then renamed after Babylonian gods—Shadrach, Meshach, and Abednego—they landed in a fiery furnace without delivery. But they were protected while inside that oven. The truth is, God can deliver us, yet like these three men, we may not always receive His delivery from hardship and suffering.

1. Read the listing in Hebrews 11:35–38 of the godly who endured torture and affliction, some destitute of health and clothing, some even losing their lives. Their faithfulness to God is given as an example. In your opinion, what allowed them to endure through loss of comfort, status, and reputation as they were maligned?

2. Which of those three losses—comfort, status, or reputation—would be most difficult for you to forego, and why?

Persecution and the Helper

The Holy Spirit plays an important role in assisting Christians as they endure persecution and loss. The Spirit helps us when in our pain and weakness we do not know what to pray. The Spirit's groanings (Rom. 8:26) during our suffering are known and understood by God the Father so that these deep yearnings are communicated to Him. In addition, as our Helper, the Spirit "gives us the right words when we stand before our persecutors" to testify about Christ.

3. To what extent do you welcome the Holy Spirit into your prayer life when you feel great pain or sense you are unable to pray clearly? If you feel limited in your prayer life and sense distance from or frustration with God during times of loss or suffering, admit this to Him. Thank Him for the gift of the Holy Spirit. Then in honesty before the Spirit, express any feelings of fear or pain. Words may be few and may lack eloquence, but the Spirit who senses them will give you comfort and communicate your feelings to an all-knowing, compassionate God.

PONDER AND DISCUSS

We need to ask Him for [wisdom]. Not once or twice but every time we face angry enemies. God is the storehouse of wisdom, and since we lack it, we need to regularly request more from Him. He gives to us "without reproach," (James 1:5) so we need not fear He'll be critical if we continually ask for more.

1. Dr. Nyquist adds that wisdom allows us "to rightly respond" to a situation. Have you ever prayed for God's wisdom before or during a meeting with someone you sensed (or knew) would be hostile to you personally in *any* situation (not just your Christian belief)? If so, what happened? (If not, be aware of this resource for wisdom and look for an opportunity to so pray before your next meeting.)

2. If your answer to the above question is yes, what was your attitude toward their words and to them personally as you listened?

The writer of Hebrews [in Heb. 12:1–2] desires his readers—and us— to run the race of the Christian life with endurance, despite continued persecution. How? He lists three strategic decisions we must make . . . remember the heroes . . . drop the weights . . . and keep looking at Christ.

3. Of the three decisions we must make to increase our endurance against opposition to our Christian faith, which one is most challenging for (or neglected by) you? Is it (1) remembering the example and encouragement of the heroes who walked by faith; (2) dropping the weights (sins and bad habits) that slow us; or (3) looking regularly to Jesus for strength and as a model to follow? Why is this difficult to do? Pray for an awareness through the Spirit when you are struggling in that area this week, as well as God's help. If you are part of a discussion group, reveal which is the most challenging decision for you and ask people in your group to pray for you this week. Then pray this week for them, for alertness and change in the area where they struggle.

9

AN ENCOURAGING WORD FROM THE PERSECUTED CHURCH

THE ISSUES

Persecution in Pakistan

The events of chapter 9 alternate from repulsive to inspiring as a leader in the Pakistani church recounts incidents of physical, social, and economic loss for Christians who remain faithful despite laws in Pakistan that make them second-class citizens in a Muslim dominated country. Both churches and the faith of individuals grow in spite of persecution.

The unnamed writer first experienced religious discrimination in fifth grade. Seeking water at summer school on a hot June day he approached the water jar for a drink. The bottle was shared among Muslim students, and when he sought a drink they rose in anger and severely beat the boy. When he returned home he asked his father why he had to endure such pain.

1. What did his father say in response to the question? If you were asked that question by someone under persecution, would you say the same thing, or perhaps give a different reminder of God's fundamental goodness and compassion?

If you felt anger, how would you deal with it—or help your friend to deal with it?

From Pakistan to America

In a litany of suffering and abuse heaped among believers in parts of Pakistan, Nyquist describes a government that wants only Christians working at low-paying cleaning jobs; brick makers who are paid little and have debts deceitfully recorded; a Christian high school teacher forced to leave his job after being accused of blasphemy against Islam (and later "invited" to leave the country by a judge); a Muslim mob that attacked five different Christian communities, burning down houses; and a Christian mother and a Christian nurse raped by Muslim men.

Although Christians in America do not face this kind of persecution from other religious groups, there is evidence of anti-Christian sentiment, such as in the media and by economic boycotts, threats of jail, and censure to Christian businesses and merchants who resist municipal and federal law because they believe those laws violate God's laws.

2. In chapter 5 Nyquist mentioned that one day churches may be forced to perform same-sex marriages or face loss of their tax-exempt status, and Bible colleges may be asked to hire transgender faculty applicants or lose their accreditation. Do you think Christians may face legal, economic, or social opposition in other areas in the future? If so, in what forms will such persecution take place?

PONDER AND DISCUSS

After two explosions ripped through a crowd departing the Peshawar All Saints Church in 2013, killing more than eighty, other churches raised financial support for wheelchairs, food supplies, first-aid kits, and relocating the injured to medical facilities. The results of the vicious attack were surprising, notes a leader of the Pakistani church:

God paved the way for us to turn persecution into an opportunity to share the gospel. The youth and other volunteers distributed one Bible per household with food supplies. With each first-aid kit we included Christian literature in local languages. All of this suffering seems trivial in hindsight. Not only did our ministry grow tenfold, but there was tremendous growth in the Pakistani church.

1. Despite the stories of a persecuted church in Pakistan that includes job loss, poor pay, personal attacks, and even bombings, God receives glory and the gospel is spread though churches and people are attacked. What do you find most impressive or surprising about this outcome in Peshawar, Pakistan?

Through every trial and hardship, Pakistani believers have emerged stronger in faith. Persecution also brought many seekers and converts, thus causing the Church to grow in ways that would not have been possible if there had not been persecution.

2. The story of the conversion of Mr. HM from Islam to Christianity is striking. What part of this story most impresses you?

10

THE HOPE
OF REVIVAL

———

THE ISSUES

Revival

In this final chapter of hope in the midst of times increasingly hostile to Christians, Nyquist declares, "We desperately need a fresh wave of God's Spirit to crash across America." He calls for revival to awaken and enliven the people of the United States. He offers two precise definitions of revival, one by Harold J. Ockenga and one by J. Edwin Orr.

1. Do either of these definitions surprise you? If so, how do they differ from your understanding of what revival is? (Notice that Ockenga's definition focuses on the spiritually lost and their attitudes toward God, while Orr's definition adds to it the revival of the believers who become involved in "evangelism, teaching, and social change.")

A history of five revivals in America, beginning in the colonial times and spanning 215 years (1725–1940), may seem like lengthy, detailed history, but those revivals contain stories of lives changed in challenging, difficult times—the final awakening ended as World War II loomed. Each revival also brought beneficial changes, with new hospitals, colleges, and youth organizations.

2. Review the five awakenings. Choose two that stand out in terms of changes in people and society. What most impresses you about those two periods of revival? Share your impressions with your group. Then thank God for His power to change lives.

There are six characteristics of revivals we are to keep in mind: (1) spiritual progress is never steady; (2) revivals are periodic but not predictable; (3) revivals follow pitiful seasons in the church; (4) a leader emerges who incarnates the revival message; (5) revival rolls irresistibly over the land; and (6) the nation is transformed for good.

3. Of the first five characteristics of revival which are most encouraging? Why? Thank God for His care for His people.

PONDER AND DISCUSS

Can [revival] happen? Revival is God's work, and our God has not lost one ounce of His power. This is kid's stuff to Him. Will it happen? That's the key question. . . . . I don't know if it will.

1. Do you think revival will come to America? Why or why not? In your answer, consider your own attitudes toward and experiences with other Christians and churches. Would you describe your feelings toward spiritual revival as cynical, cautious, or anticipating God's power in action? Be honest. If you are in a study group, compare your attitudes with those of others. Then pray, asking God to give you an openness to revival, and even a desire for revival in your life and in America.

In the closing pages of this chapter, Dr. Nyquist reminds us that while only God knows His plans, we may move His hands:

If we humbly confess, fervently pray, vibrantly believe, and boldly evangelize, will revival come? Only our sovereign God knows. . . . If God graciously visits this land in a powerful way, the current cultural trends will be immediately arrested, biblical values will return, and the threat of persecution will disappear. And you won't need this book.

Confessing, praying, believing, and evangelizing may spark revival, but these activities don't comprise a formula for revival. Nyquist again reminds us that only God knows if revival will come. Still, he writes, "I am encouraged by how God answered His people the last time we cried to Him," a reference to the Eisenhower revival of 1949–1960.

2. Which of these four activities is/are most lacking in your life? Ask God to help you develop zeal in those areas. Spiritual revival often begins in our own hearts, so let it begin in yours. And then pray that through God's Holy Spirit revival may spread through America. Then indeed the persecution can diminish—and God will be honored once more.

AFTERWORD

———

THE ISSUES

Preparing for Coming Persecution

1. Although spiritual revival may come, without it Christians can expect increasing antagonism in the future. Such antagonism will attack both our belief system and us personally. What do you think the "physical, emotional, and financial effects" will include?

2. To prepare for these attacks, we are to do three things: be _____, be _____, and be _____. As a result of reading *Prepare*, which of these three do you feel most ready for? What can you do to prepare in the other two areas?

When we encounter persecution, the Bible gives us three options. We can flee from it, we can defend ourselves, or we can stand firm. Yet in all three options we need not fear persecution (see Matt. 10:26, 28; 1 Peter 3:14–15). At first glance it would seem the option of fleeing would be an act of fear. Yet Nyquist writes "sometimes the appropriate action is to remove yourself from the hostile situation."

3. What is the criterion to decide whether we should flee or stay in persecution, according to the final two paragraphs before the section "Defend Ourselves"? What does this tell you about God's plans for us?

4. Even when we apply the criterion, the decision may feel unclear, either because of our feelings, or by seemingly complicating the situation. At that point, we need wisdom. What should we do next and what is the promise of God, according to James 1:5?

5. Think of missionaries in countries where persecution exists and pray on their behalf for wisdom in their daily contacts.

PONDER AND DISCUSS

*Not knowing what awaits us, we can worry about failure. What if we
fail miserably in the face of persecution? What if we dishonor our Lord
in our actions and attitudes despite our best intentions?
None of us wants to fail, but at some point it's inevitable.*

1. It may be a surprising reminder: under persecution, we at
   some point will fail in our actions or attitudes despite our
   best intentions. Does that reality disappoint you? Is there
   anything you can do to prepare for that reality—or prevent it
   from happening? What can we do when it happens?

2. The classic example of failing under persecution is Peter, who
   denied Jesus three times after boasting "I will never fall away."
   Why do we have confidence before persecution, and why are
   we vulnerable to failing during the persecution and ridicule?

*What should we do when we fail our Lord? Get up. Get back up, confess
our failure, and stay in the race knowing God wants to restore us and
use us. He didn't leave Peter in the dumps, and He won't leave us there
either.*

3. The third sentence really answers the final question under
   question 1 above: "What can we do when it [our failure]
   happens?" Why is it so difficult to confess and then stay in

the race? What hope can you take from Jesus' restoration of Peter after that disciple's colossal failure?

Peter reminds us of what God will do for us . . . when he writes, "After you have suffered a little while, the God of all grace, who has called you to his eternal glory in Christ, will himself restore, confirm, strengthen, and establish you (1 Peter 5:10).

4. That Bible promise comes from the disciple who experienced it after he denied his relationship with Jesus three times. Make this promise personal—what does it mean to you? Then this week memorize this promise, and ask God to give you strength.

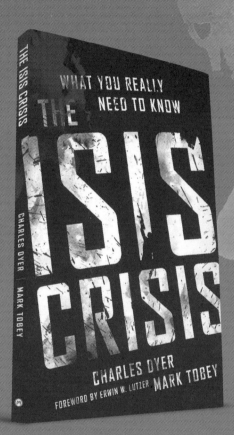

Tune in each weekday to **In the Market with Janet Parshall**. Janet and highly respected guests examine news stories and issues in the marketplace of ideas using the Bible as a framework for discussion. Enjoy an engaging mix of commentary and listener interaction.

www.inthemarketwithjanetparshall.org

MOODY Radio™

*From the Word **to Life***